A Taste of
Chicken Soup for the Soul®

Chicken Soup for the Soul

20th Anniversary Edition

Stories to Open the Heart and
Rekindle the Spirit

Jack Canfield
Mark Victor Hansen
Amy Newmark

CSS

Chicken Soup for the Soul Publishing, LLC
Cos Cob, CT

A Taste of Chicken Soup for the Soul: 20th Anniversary Edition
Stories to Open the Heart and Rekindle the Spirit
Jack Canfield, Mark Victor Hansen & Amy Newmark

Published by Chicken Soup for the Soul Publishing, LLC
www.chickensoup.com

The publisher gratefully acknowledges the many publishers and
individuals who granted Chicken Soup for the Soul permission to
reprint the cited material.

Library of Congress Control Number: 2013937402

A Taste of ISBN: 978-1-61159-866-7

Full Book ISBN: 978-1-61159-913-8

Contents

The Hugging Judge

Lee Shapiro is a retired judge. He is also one of the most genuinely loving people we know. At one point in his career, Lee realized that love is the greatest power there is. As a result, Lee became a hugger. He began offering everybody a hug. His colleagues dubbed him "the hugging judge" (as opposed to the hanging judge, we suppose). The bumper sticker on his car reads, "Don't bug me! Hug me!"

About six years ago Lee created what he calls his Hugger Kit. On the outside it reads "A heart for a hug." The inside contains 30 little red embroidered hearts with stickums on the back. Lee will take out his Hugger Kit, go around to people and offer them a little red heart in exchange for a hug.

Lee has become so well known for this that

he is often invited to keynote conferences and conventions, where he shares his message of unconditional love. At a conference in San Francisco, the local news media challenged him by saying, "It is easy to give out hugs here in the conference to people who self-selected to be here. But this would never work in the real world."

They challenged Lee to give away some hugs on the streets of San Francisco. Followed by a television crew from the local news station, Lee went out onto the street. First he approached a woman walking by. "Hi, I'm Lee Shapiro, the hugging judge. I'm giving out these hearts in exchange for a hug." "Sure," she replied. "Too easy," challenged the local commentator. Lee looked around. He saw a meter maid who was being given a hard time by the owner of a BMW to whom she was giving a ticket. He marched up to her, camera crew in tow, and said, "You look like you could use a hug. I'm the hugging judge and I'm offering you one." She accepted.

The television commentator threw down one final challenge. "Look, here comes a bus. San Francisco bus drivers are the toughest people in the whole town. Let's see you get him to hug you." Lee took the challenge.

As the bus pulled up to the curb, Lee said, "Hi, I'm Lee Shapiro, the hugging judge. This has got to be one of the most stressful jobs in the whole world. I'm offering hugs to people today to lighten the load a little. Would you like one?" The six-foot-two, 230-pound bus driver got out of his seat, stepped down and said, "Why not?"

Lee hugged him, gave him a heart and waved goodbye as the bus pulled out. The TV crew was speechless. Finally, the commentator said, "I have to admit, I'm very impressed."

One day, Lee's friend Nancy Johnston showed up on his doorstep. Nancy is a professional clown and she was wearing her clown costume, make-up and all. "Lee, grab a bunch of your Hugger Kits and let's go out to the home for the disabled."

When they arrived at the home, they started giving out balloon hats, hearts and hugs to the patients. Lee was uncomfortable. He had never before hugged people who were terminally ill, severely retarded or quadriplegic. It was definitely a stretch. But after a while it became easier, with Nancy and Lee acquiring an entourage of doctors, nurses and orderlies who followed them from ward to ward.

After several hours they entered the last ward. These were 34 of the worst cases Lee had seen in his life. The feeling was so grim it took his heart away. But because of their commitment to share their love and to make a difference, Nancy and Lee started working their way around the room followed by the entourage of medical staff, all of whom by now had hearts on their collars and balloon hats on their heads.

Finally, Lee came to the last person, Leonard. Leonard was wearing a big white bib, which he was drooling on. Lee looked at Leonard dribbling onto his bib and said, "Let's go, Nancy. There's no way we can get through to this person." Nancy replied, "C'mon, Lee. He's a fellow human being, too, isn't he?" Then she placed a funny balloon hat on his head. Lee took one of his little red hearts and placed it on Leonard's bib. He took a deep breath, leaned down and gave Leonard a hug.

All of a sudden Leonard began to squeal, "Eeeeehh! Eeeeeehh!" Some of the other patients in the room began to clang things together. Lee turned to the staff for some sort of explanation only to find that every doctor, nurse and orderly was crying. Lee asked the head nurse, "What's going on?"

Lee will never forget what she said: "This is the first time in 23 years we've seen Leonard smile."

How simple it is to make a difference in the lives of others.

~Jack Canfield and Mark Victor Hansen

The Two Saddest Words

Two of the saddest words in the English language are "if only." I live my life with the goal of never having to say those words, because they convey regret, lost opportunities, mistakes, and disappointment. And sometimes the words "if only" go with terrible tragedies. Think about how many times you have heard about something awful happening, accompanied by "if only he had called her back to make sure she was okay ..." or "if only I had investigated that noise ..." or "if only they had made sure the gate to the pool clicked behind them..."

My father-in-law is famous in our family for saying, "Take the extra minute to do it right." He must be doing something right, since he's 91 years old and still making a lot of sense.

I always try to live by the "extra minute" rule. Sometimes it only takes seconds to make sure I write something down correctly, or check something on the Internet, or move an object out of the way before it trips someone. And of course when my children were young, and prone to all kinds of mishaps, I lived and breathed the extra minute rule. I always thought about what I could do to avoid an "if only" moment, whether it was something minor like moving a cup full of hot coffee away from the edge of a counter, or something that required a little more work such as taping padding onto the sharp corners of a glass coffee table.

I just read a news story about a student pilot who was thrown from an airplane when its canopy lifted off. The instructor, who was belted in, was fine. The student, whose seatbelt was not fastened, fell from the sky and his body was found on the ground somewhere in Tennessee. Imagine how many people are in mourning, and how terrified that man must have been as he fell from the plane and realized he was going to die. Imagine the chorus of "if only" coming from his family. If only he had been wearing his seatbelt... How simple would that have been?

I don't move my car one inch until I hear the seatbelt click on every passenger. I unplug the iron when I leave the laundry room for "just a minute." I'd hate to get distracted, not return to the laundry room, and start a fire with that forgotten iron. Imagine the "if only" I'd be saying then. After I realized that I could not be trusted with a teakettle — I left it boiling on the stove for an hour — I threw it out and bought an electric teakettle that shuts itself off. And I am paranoid about fireplace ashes. I wait till they are two weeks old, then shovel them into a bag on garbage collection day and put the bag 20 feet away from the house in the middle of the driveway.

When my teenage son was first driving, I worried that enforcing his curfew too strictly would cause him to speed and have an accident. A boy in the next town was killed when he drove too fast trying to make it home by midnight. So my son and I agreed on a plan — if he missed curfew he would just lose double those minutes the next night out. Ten minutes late meant 20 minutes shaved off the curfew the next time, consequences that were not so onerous that they would cause him to rush home.

When I was in a car accident a few years ago, resulting in spinal surgery and permanent nerve damage, I handled it well emotionally, because I wasn't the driver who was at fault. There was no "if only" thinking for me, and it's a lot easier to forgive someone else than it is to forgive yourself.

I don't only avoid those "if only" moments when it comes to safety. It's equally important to avoid "if only" in our personal relationships. We all know people who lost a loved one and bemoaned the fact that they had foregone an opportunity to say "I love you" or "I forgive you." When my father announced he was going to the eye doctor across from my office on Good Friday, I told him that it was a holiday for Chicken Soup for the Soul and I wouldn't be here. But then I thought about the fact that he's 84 years old and I realized that I shouldn't give up an opportunity to see him. I called him and told him I had decided to go to work on my day off after all. When my husband's beloved, elderly uncle pocket-dialed me several times yesterday with his new cell phone, I urged my husband to call him back, invoking the "if only" possibility. My husband called him and was glad that he did. Now if anything happens, my husband won't have to say, "If only I had called him back that day."

I know there will still be occasions when I have to say "if only" about something, but my life is definitely more serene because of my policy of doing everything possible to avoid that eventuality. And even though it takes an extra minute to do something right, or it occasionally takes an hour or two in my busy schedule to make a personal connection, I know that I'm doing the right thing. I'm buying myself peace of mind and that's the best kind of insurance for my emotional wellbeing.

~Amy Newmark

Who You Are
Makes a Difference

A teacher in New York decided to honor her seniors in high school by telling them the difference they each made. Using a process developed by Helice Bridges of Del Mar, California, she called each student to the front of the class, one at a time. First she told them they made a difference to her and the class. Then she presented each of them with a blue ribbon imprinted with gold letters that read, "Who I Am Makes a Difference."

Afterwards the teacher decided to do a class project to see what kind of impact recognition would have on a community. She gave each of the students three more ribbons and instructed them to go out and spread this acknowledgment ceremony. Then they were to follow up on the results, see who honored whom and report back to the class in about a week.

One of the boys in the class went to a junior executive in a nearby company and honored him for helping him with his career planning. He gave him a blue ribbon and put it on his shirt. Then he gave him two extra ribbons, and said, "We're doing a class project on recognition, and we'd like you to go out, find somebody to honor, give them a blue ribbon, then give them the extra blue ribbon so they can acknowledge a third person to keep this acknowledgment ceremony going. Then please report back to me and tell me what happened."

Later that day the junior executive went in to see his boss, who had been noted, by the way, as being kind of a grouchy fellow. He sat his boss down and he told him that he deeply admired him for being a creative genius. The boss seemed very surprised. The junior executive asked him if he would accept the gift of the blue ribbon and give him permission to put it on him. His surprised boss said, "Well, sure."

The junior executive took the blue ribbon and placed it right on his boss's jacket above his heart. As he gave him the last extra ribbon, he said, "Would you do me a favor? Would you take this extra ribbon and pass it on by honoring somebody else? The young boy who first gave me the ribbons is doing a project in school and we want to keep this recognition ceremony going and find out how it affects people."

That night the boss went home to his 14-year-old son and sat him down. He said, "The most incredible thing happened to me today. I was in my office and one of the junior executives came in and told me he admired me and gave me a blue ribbon for being a creative genius. Imagine. He thinks I'm a creative genius. Then he put this blue ribbon that says 'Who I Am Makes a Difference' on my jacket above my heart. He gave me an extra ribbon and asked me to find somebody else to honor. As I was driving home tonight, I started thinking about whom I would honor with this ribbon and I thought about you. I want to honor you.

"My days are really hectic and when I come home I don't pay a lot of attention to you. Sometimes I scream at you for not getting good enough grades in school and for your bedroom being a mess, but somehow tonight, I just wanted to sit here and, well, just let you know that you do make a difference to me. Besides your mother, you are the most important person in my life. You're a great kid and I love you!"

The startled boy started to sob and sob, and he couldn't stop crying. His whole body shook. He looked up at his father and said through his tears, "I was planning on committing suicide tomorrow, Dad, because I didn't think you loved me. Now I don't need to."

~Helice Bridges

Love and the Cabbie

I was in New York the other day and rode with a friend in a taxi. When we got out, my friend said to the driver, "Thank you for the ride. You did a superb job of driving."

The taxi driver was stunned for a second. Then he said, "Are you a wise guy or something?"

"No, my dear man, and I'm not putting you on. I admire the way you keep cool in heavy traffic."

"Yeah," the driver said and drove off.

"What was that all about?" I asked.

"I am trying to bring love back to New York," he said. "I believe it's the only thing that can save the city."

"How can one man save New York?"

"It's not one man. I believe I have made

that taxi driver's day. Suppose he has 20 fares. He's going to be nice to those 20 fares because someone was nice to him. Those fares in turn will be kinder to their employees or shopkeepers or waiters or even their own families. Eventually the goodwill could spread to at least 1,000 people. Now that isn't bad, is it?"

"But you're depending on that taxi driver to pass your goodwill to others."

"I'm not depending on it," my friend said. "I'm aware that the system isn't foolproof so I might deal with 10 different people today. If out of 10 I can make three happy, then eventually I can indirectly influence the attitudes of 3,000 more."

"It sounds good on paper," I admitted, "but I'm not sure it works in practice."

"Nothing is lost if it doesn't. It didn't take any of my time to tell that man he was doing a good job. He neither received a larger tip nor a smaller tip. If it fell on deaf ears, so what? Tomorrow there will be another taxi driver I can try to make happy."

"You're some kind of a nut," I said.

"That shows how cynical you have become. I have made a study of this. The thing that seems to be lacking, besides money of course, for our postal employees, is that no one tells people who work for the post office what a good job they're doing."

"But they're not doing a good job."

"They're not doing a good job because they feel no one cares if they do or not. Why shouldn't someone say a kind word to them?"

We were walking past a structure in the process of being built and passed five workmen eating their lunch. My friend stopped. "That's a magnificent job you men have done. It must be difficult and dangerous work."

The workmen eyed my friend suspiciously.

"When will it be finished?"

"June," a man grunted.

"Ah. That really is impressive. You must all be very proud."

We walked away. I said to him, "I haven't seen anyone like you since *Man of La Mancha.*"

"When those men digest my words, they will feel better for it. Somehow the city will benefit from their happiness."

"But you can't do this all alone!" I protested. "You're just one man."

"The most important thing is not to get discouraged. Making people in the city become kind again is not an easy job, but if I can enlist other people in my campaign..."

"You just winked at a very plain-looking woman," I said.

"Yes, I know," he replied. "And if she's a schoolteacher, her class will be in for a fantastic day."

~Art Buchwald

I Know You, You're Just Like Me!

One of our closest friends is Stan Dale. Stan teaches a seminar on love and relationships called "Sex, Love and Intimacy." Several years ago, in an effort to learn what the people in the Soviet Union were really like, he took 29 people to the Soviet Union for two weeks. When he wrote about his experiences in his newsletter, we were deeply touched by the following anecdote:

While walking through a park in the industrial city of Kharkov, I spotted an old Russian veteran of World War II. They are easily identified by the medals and ribbons they still proudly display on their shirts and jackets.

This is not an act of egotism. It is their country's way of honoring those who helped save Russia, even though 20 million Russians were killed by the Nazis. I went up to this old man sitting with his wife and said, "Druzhba i mir" (friendship and peace). The man looking at me as if in disbelief, took the button we had made for the trip and said "Friendship" in Russian and showed a map of the U.S. and the U.S.S.R. being held by loving hands, and said, "Americanski?" I replied, "Da, Americanski. Druzhba i mir." He clasped both my hands as if we were long lost brothers and repeated again, "Americanski!" This time there was recognition and love in his statement.

For the next few minutes he and his wife spoke in Russian as if I understood every word, and I spoke English as if I knew he would understand. You know what? Neither of us understood a word, but we surely understood each other. We hugged, and laughed and cried, all the while saying, "Druzhba i mir, Americanski." "I love you, I am proud to be in your country, we do not want war. *I love you!*"

After about five minutes we said goodbye, and the seven of us in our little group walked on. About 15 minutes later, some considerable distance on, this same old veteran caught up with us. He came up to me, took off his Order of Lenin medal (probably his most prized possession) and pinned it to my jacket. He then kissed me on the lips and gave me one of the warmest, most loving hugs I have ever received. Then we both cried, looked into each other's eyes for the longest time, and said, "Dossvedanya" (goodbye).

The above story is symbolic of our entire "Citizen Diplomacy" trip to the Soviet Union. Every day we met and touched hundreds of people in every possible and impossible setting. Neither the Russians nor we will ever be the same. There are now hundreds of schoolchildren from the three schools we visited who will not be quite so ready to think of Americans as people who want to "nuke" them. We danced, sang and played with children of every age, and then we hugged, kissed and shared presents. They gave us flowers, cakes, buttons, paintings, dolls, but most importantly, their hearts and open minds.

More than once we were invited to be members of wedding parties, and no biological family member could have been more warmly accepted, greeted and feted than we were. We hugged, kissed, danced and drank champagne, schnapps and vodka with the bride and groom, as well as Momma and Poppa and the rest of the family.

In Kursk, we were hosted by seven Russian families who volunteered to take us in for a wonderful evening of food, drink and conversation. Four hours later, none of us wanted to part. Our group now has a complete new family in Russia.

The following night "our family" was feted by us at our hotel. The band played until almost midnight, and guess what? Once again we ate, drank, talked, danced and cried when it came time to say goodbye. We danced every dance as if we were passionate lovers, which is exactly what we were.

I could go on forever about our experiences, and yet there would be no way to convey to you exactly how we felt. How would you feel when you arrived at your hotel in Moscow, if there were a telephone message waiting for you, written in Russian, from Mikhail Gorbachev's office saying he regretted he could not meet with you that weekend because he would be out of town, but instead he had arranged for your entire group to meet for two hours in a roundtable discussion with about a half-dozen members of the Central Committee? We had an extremely frank discussion about everything, including sex.

How would you feel if more than a dozen old ladies, wearing babushkas, came down from the steps of their apartment buildings and hugged and kissed you? How would you feel when your guides, Tanya and Natasha, told you and the whole group that they had never seen anyone like you? And when we left, all 30 of us cried because we had fallen in love with these fabulous women, and they with us. Yes, how would you feel? Probably just like us.

Each of us had our own experience, of course, but the collective experience bears out one thing for certain: The only way we are ever going to ensure peace on this planet is to adopt the entire world as "our family." We are going to have to hug them, and kiss them. And dance and play with them. And we are going to have to sit and talk and walk and cry with them. Because when we do, we'll be able to see that, indeed, everyone is beautiful, and we all complement each other so beautifully, and we would all be poorer without each other. Then the saying, "I know you, you're just like me!" will take on a mega-meaning of, "This is 'my family,' and I will stand by them no matter what!"

~Stan Dale

Just Say It!

One night, after reading one of the hundreds of parenting books I've read, I was feeling a little guilty because the book had described some parenting strategies I hadn't used in a while. The main strategy was to talk with your child and use those three magic words: "I love you." It had stressed over and over that children need to know unconditionally and unequivocally that you really love them.

I went upstairs to my son's bedroom and knocked on the door. As I knocked, all I could hear were his drums. I knew he was there but he wasn't answering. So I opened the door and, sure enough, there he was sitting with his earphones on, listening to a tape and playing his drums. After I leaned over to get his attention, I said to him, "Tim, have you got a second?"

He said, "Oh sure, Dad. I'm always good for one." We proceeded to sit down and after about 15 minutes and a lot of small talk and stuttering, I just looked at him and said,

"Tim, I really love the way you play drums."

He said, "Oh, thanks, Dad, I appreciate it."

I walked out the door and said, "See you later!" As I was walking downstairs, it dawned on me that I went up there with a certain message and had not delivered it. I felt it was really important to get back up there and have another chance to say those three magic words.

Again I climbed the stairs, knocked on the door and opened it. "You got a second, Tim?"

"Sure, Dad. I'm always good for a second or two. What do you need?"

"Son, the first time I came up here to share a message with you, something else came out. It really wasn't what I wanted to share with you. Tim, do you remember when you were learning how to drive, it caused me a lot of problems? I wrote three words and slipped them under your pillow in hopes that would take care of it. I'd done my part as a parent and expressed my love to my son." Finally after a little small talk, I looked at Tim and said, "What I want you to know is that we love you."

He looked at me and said, "Oh, thanks, Dad. That's you and Mom?"

I said, "Yeah, that's both of us, we just don't express it enough."

He said, "Thanks, that means a lot. I know you do."

I turned around and walked out the door. As I was walking downstairs, I started thinking, "I can't believe this. I've already been up there twice — I know what the message is and yet something else comes out of my mouth."

I decided I'm going back there now and let Tim know exactly how I feel. He's going to hear it directly from me. I don't care if he is six feet tall! So back I go, knock on the door and he yells "Wait a minute. Don't tell me who it is. Could that be you, Dad?"

I said, "How'd you know that?" and he responded, "I've known you ever since you were a parent, Dad."

Then I said "Son, have you got just one more second?"

"You know I'm good for one, so come on in. I suppose you didn't tell me what you wanted to tell me?"

I said, "How'd you know that?"

"I've known you ever since I was in diapers."

I said, "Well, here it is, Tim, what I've been holding back on. I just want to express to you how special you are to our family. It's not what you do, and it's not what you've done, like all the things you're doing with the junior high kids in town. It's who you are as a person. I love you and I just wanted you to know I love you, and I don't know why I hold back on something so important."

He looked at me and he said, "Hey, Dad, I know you do and it's really special hearing you say it to me. Thanks so much for your thoughts, as well as the intent." As I was walking out the door, he said, "Oh, hey, Dad. Have you got another second?"

I started thinking, "Oh no. What's he going to say to me?" I said, "Oh sure. I'm always good for one."

I don't know where kids get this — I'm sure it couldn't be from their parents, but he said, "Dad, I just want to ask you one question."

I said, "What's that?"

He looked at me and said, "Dad, have you been to a workshop or something like that?"

I'm thinking, "Oh no, like any other 18-year-old, he's got my number," and I said,

"No, I was reading a book, and it said how important it is to tell your kids how you really feel about them."

"Hey, thanks for taking the time. Talk to you later, Dad."

I think what Tim taught me, more than anything else that night is that the only way you can understand the real meaning and purpose of love is to be willing to pay the price. You have to go out there and risk sharing it.

~Gene Bedley

The Perfect American Family

It is 10:30 on a perfect Saturday morning and we are, for the moment, the perfect American family. My wife has taken our six-year-old to his first piano lesson. Our 14-year-old has not yet roused from his slumber. The four-year-old watches tiny, anthropomorphic beings hurl one another from cliffs in the other room. I sit at the kitchen table reading the newspaper.

Aaron Malachi, the four-year-old, apparently bored by the cartoon carnage and the considerable personal power obtained by holding the television's remote control, enters my space.

"I'm hungry," he says.

"Want some more cereal?"

"No."

"Want some yogurt?"

"No."

"Want some eggs?"

"No. Can I have some ice cream?"

"No."

For all I know, ice cream may be far more nourishing than processed cereal or antibiotic-laden eggs but, according to my cultural values, it is wrong to have ice cream at 10:45 on a Saturday morning.

Silence. About four seconds. "Daddy, we have very much of life left, don't we?"

"Yes, we have lots of life left, Aaron."

"Me and you and Mommy?"

"That's right."

"And Isaac?"

"Yes."

"And Ben?"

"Yes. You and me and Mommy and Isaac and Ben."

"We have very much of life left. Until all the people die."

"What do you mean?"

"Until all the people die and the dinosaurs come back."

Aaron sits down on the table, cross-legged like a Buddha, in the center of my newspaper.

"What do you mean, Aaron, 'until all the people die'?"

"You said everybody dies. When everybody dies, then the dinosaurs will come back. The cavemen lived in caves, dinosaur caves. Then the dinosaurs came back and squished 'em."

I realize that already for Aaron life is a limited economy, a resource with a beginning and an end. He envisions himself and us somewhere along that trajectory, a trajectory that ends in uncertainty and loss.

I am faced with an ethical decision. What should I do now? Should I attempt to give him God, salvation, eternity? Should I toss him some spiel like, "Your body is just a shell and after you die, we will all be together in spirit forever"?

Or should I leave him with his uncertainty

and his anxiety because I think it's real? Should I try to make him an anxious existentialist or should I try to make him feel better?

I don't know. I stare at the newspaper. The Celtics are consistently losing on Friday nights. Larry Bird is angry at somebody, but I can't see who, because Aaron's foot is in the way. I don't know but my neurotic, addictive, middle-class sensibility is telling me that this is a very important moment, a moment when Aaron's ways of constructing his world are being formed. Or maybe my neurotic, addictive, middle-class sensibility is just making me think that. If life and death are an illusion, then why should I trifle with how someone else understands them?

On the table Aaron plays with an "army guy," raising his arms and balancing him on his shaky legs. It was Kevin McHale that Larry Bird was angry at. No, not Kevin McHale, it was Jerry Sichting. But Jerry Sichting is no longer with the Celtics. Whatever happened to Jerry Sichting? Everything dies; everything comes to an end. Jerry Sichting is playing for Sacramento or Orlando or he has disappeared.

I should not trifle with how Aaron understands life and death because I want him to have a solid sense of structure, a sense of the permanence of things. It's obvious what a good job the nuns and priests did with me. It was agony or bliss. Heaven and hell were not connected by long distance service. You were on God's team or you were in the soup, and the soup was hot. I don't want Aaron to get burned, but I want him to have a strong frame. The neurotic but unavoidable anxiety can come later.

Is that possible? It is possible to have a sense that God, spirit, karma, Y*H*W*H, something — is transcendent, without traumatizing the presentness of a person, without beating it into them? Can we have our cake and eat it too, ontologically speaking? Or is their fragile sensibility, their "there-ness," sundered by such an act?

Sensing a slight increase in agitation on the

table, I know that Aaron is becoming bored with his guy. With an attitude of drama benefiting the moment, I clear my throat and begin with a professional tone.

"Aaron, death is something that some people believe …."

"Dad," Aaron interrupts, "could we play a video game? It's not a very violent game," he explains, hands gesticulating. "It's not like a killing game. The guys just kind of flop over."

"Yes," I say with some relief, "let's play video games. But first there's something else we have to do."

"What?" Aaron stops and turns from where he has run, already halfway to the arcade.

"First, let's have some ice cream."

Another perfect Saturday for a perfect family. For now.

~Michael Murphy

If You Don't Ask, You Don't Get — But If You Do, You Do

My wife Linda and I live in Miami, Florida. When we had just started our self-esteem training program called Little Acorns to teach children how to say no to drugs, sexual promiscuity and other self-destructive behavior, we received a brochure for an educational conference in San Diego. As we read the brochure and realized that everybody who is anybody was going to be there, we realized we had to go. But we didn't see how. We were just getting started, we were working out of our home and we had just about exhausted our personal savings with the early stages of the work. There was no way we could afford the airline tickets or any of the other expenses. But we knew we had to be there, so we started asking.

The first thing I did was to call the conference coordinators in San Diego, explain why we just had to be there and ask them if they would give us two complimentary admissions to the conference. When I explained our situation, what we were doing and why we had to be there, they said yes. So now we had the tickets.

I told Linda we had the tickets and we could get into the conference. She said, "Great! But we're in Miami and the conference is in San Diego. What do we do next?"

So I said, "We've got to get transportation." I called an airline I knew was doing well at the time, Northeast Airlines. The woman who answered happened to be the secretary to the president so I told her what I needed. She put me directly through to the president, Steve Quinto. I explained to him that I had just talked to the conference people in San Diego, they had given us free tickets to the conference but we were stuck on how to get there and would he please donate two round trip tickets from Miami to San Diego. He said, "Of course

I will," just like that. It was that fast and the next thing he said really floored me. He said, "Thank you for asking."

I said, "Pardon me?"

He said, "I don't often have the opportunity to do the best thing that I can for the world unless someone asks me to. The best thing I can ever do is to give of myself and you've asked me to do that. That's a nice opportunity and I want to thank you for that opportunity." I was blown away, but I thanked him and hung up the phone. I looked at my wife and said, "Honey, we got the plane tickets." She said, "Great! Where do we stay?"

Next I called the Holiday Inn Downtown Miami and asked, "Where is your headquarters?" They told me it was in Memphis, Tennessee, so I called Tennessee and they patched me through to the person I needed to talk to. It was a guy in San Francisco. He controlled all of the Holiday Inns in California. I then explained to him that we had obtained our plane tickets through the airlines and asked if there were some way he could help us with the lodging for the three days. He asked if it would be okay if he put us up in their new hotel in downtown San Diego as his guest. I said, "Yes, that would be fine."

He then said, "Wait a minute. I need to caution you that the hotel is about a 35-mile drive from the campus where the conference is being held and you'll have to find out how to get there."

I said, "I'll figure it out if I need to buy a horse." I thanked him and I said to Linda, "Well, honey, we've got the admission, we've got the plane tickets and we've got a place to stay. What we need now is a way to get back and forth from the hotel to the campus twice a day."

Next I called National Car Rental, told them the story and asked if they could help me out. They said, "Would a new Olds 88 be okay?" I said it would be.

In one day we had put the whole thing together.

We did wind up buying our own meals for part of the time but before the conference was over, I stood up, told this story at one of the general assemblies and said, "Anyone who wants to volunteer to take us to lunch now and again would be graciously thanked." About 50 people jumped up and volunteered so we wound up having some of the meals thrown in as well.

We had a marvelous time, learned a lot and connected with people like Jack Canfield, who is still on our advisory board. When we returned, we launched the program and it's been growing about 100 percent a year. This last June we graduated our 2,250th family from the Little Acorn training. We've also held two major conferences for educators called *Making The World Safe For Children*, to which we've invited people from all over the world. Thousands of educators have come to get ideas on how to do self-esteem training in their classrooms while they're still teaching the three *Rs*.

The last time we sponsored the conference

we invited educators from 81 nations to come. Seventeen nations sent representatives including some ministers of education. Out of that has grown invitations for us to take our program to the following places: Russia, Ukraine, Byelorussia, Gelaruth, Kazakhstan, Mongolia, Taiwan, the Cook Islands and New Zealand.

So you see you can get anything you want if you just ask enough people.

~Rick Gelinas

Walt Jones

No one better epitomizes the fact that success is a journey and not a destination than the many green and growing "human becomings" who do not allow age to be a deterrent to accomplishment. Florence Brooks joined the Peace Corps when she was 64 years of age. Gladys Clappison was living in the dormitory at the University of Iowa working on her Ph.D. in history at age 82. Then there was Ed Stitt, who at age 87, was working on his community college degree program in New Jersey. Ed said it kept him from getting "old-timers' disease" and kept his brain alive.

Probably no one person has stirred my imagination over the years more than Walt Jones of Tacoma, Washington. Walt outlived his third wife to whom he was married for 52 years. When she died, someone said to Walt that it must be sad losing such a long-time friend. His response was, "Well, of course it was, but then again it may be for the best."

"Why was that?"

"I don't want to be negative or say anything to defame her wonderful character, but she kind of petered out on me in the last decade."

When asked to explain, he went on to add, "She just never wanted to do nothin', just kind of became a stick-in-the-mud. Ten years ago when I was 94, I told my wife we ain't never seen nothin' except the beautiful Pacific Northwest. She asked me what was on my mind, and I told her I was thinkin' about buying a motor home and maybe we could visit all 48 of the contiguous states. 'What do you think of that?'

"She said, 'I think you're out of your mind, Walt.'

"'Whydya say that?' I asked.

"'We'd get mugged out there. We'd die

and there wouldn't be a funeral parlor.' Then she asked me, 'Who's going to drive, Walter?' and I said, 'I am, Lambie.' 'You'll kill us!' she said.

"I'd like to make footprints in the sands of time before I check out, but you can't make footprints in the sands of time if you're sitting on your butt... unless your intent is to make buttprints in the sands of time."

"So now that she's gone, Walt, what do you intend to do?"

"What do I intend to do? I buried the old gal and bought me a motor home. This is 1976, and I intend to visit all 48 of the states to celebrate our bicentennial."

Walt got to 43 of the states that year selling curios and souvenirs. When asked if he ever picked up hitchhikers, he said, "No way. Too many of them will club you over the head for four bits or sue you for whiplash if you get into an accident."

Walt hadn't had his motor home but a few months and his wife had only been buried for six months when he was seen driving down the street with a rather attractive 62-year-old woman at his side.

"Walt?" he was asked.

"Yeah," he replied.

"Who was the woman sitting by your side? Who's your new lady friend, Walt?"

To which he replied, "Yes, she is."

"Yes she is what?"

"My lady friend."

"Lady friend? Walt, you've been married three times, you're 104 years of age. This woman must be four decades younger than you."

"Well," he responded, "I quickly discovered that man cannot live in a motor home alone."

"I can understand that, Walt. You probably miss having someone to talk to after having had a companion all these years."

Without hesitation Walt replied, "You know, I miss that, too."

"Too? Are you inferring that you have a

romantic interest?"

"I just might."

"Walt ..."

"What?" he said.

"There comes a time in a person's life when you knock off that stuff."

"Sex?" he replied.

"Yes."

"Why?" he asked.

"Well, because that kind of physical exertion could be hazardous to a person's health."

Walt considered the question and said, "Well, if she dies, she dies."

In 1978 with double digit inflation heating up in our country, Walt was a major investor in a condominium development. When asked why he was taking his money out of a secure bank account and putting it into a condo development, he said, "Ain't you heard? These are inflationary times. You've got to put your money into real property so it will appreciate and be around for your later years when you really need it." How's that for positive thinking?

In 1980 he sold off a lot of his property in and around Pierce County, Washington. Many people thought Walt was cashing in his chips. He assembled his friends and quickly made it clear that he was not cashing in his chips, but he had sold off the property for cash flow. "I took a small down and a 30-year contract. I got four grand a month comin' in until I'm 138."

He celebrated his 110th birthday on the Johnny Carson Show. He walked out resplendent in his white beard and black hat looking a little like the late Colonel Sanders, and Johnny says, "It's good to have you here, Walt."

"It's good to be anywhere at 110, Johnny."

"110?"

"110."

"1-1-0?"

"What's the matter, Carson, you losin' your hearin'? That's what I said. That's what I am. What's the big deal?"

"The big deal is you're within three days of

being twice as old as I am."

That would get your attention, wouldn't it? One hundred and ten years of age — a green, growing human becoming. Walt picked up the opening and quickly alluded to Johnny.

"How old would you be if you didn't know the date you were born and there weren't no durned calendar to semi-depress you once a year? Ever heard of people getting depressed because of a calendar date? Oh, Lordy, I hit my 30th birthday. I'm so depressed, I'm over the hill. Oh, no, I hit my 40th birthday. Everybody in my work team dressed in black and sent a hearse to pick me up. Oh, no I'm 50 years old. Half a century old. They sent me dead roses with cobwebs. Johnny, who says you're supposed to roll over and die when you're 65? I have friends more prosperous since they were 75 than they were before. And as a result of a little condominium investment I made a few years ago, I've made more bucks since I was 105 than I did before. Can I give you my definition of depression, Johnny?"

"Go ahead."

"Missing a birthday."

May the story of Walt Jones inspire all of us to remain green and growing every day of our lives.

~Bob Moawad

Consider This

Consider this:

- After Fred Astaire's first screen test, the memo from the testing director of MGM, dated 1933, said, "Can't act! Slightly bald! Can dance a little!" Astaire kept that memo over the fireplace in his Beverly Hills home.

- An expert said of Vince Lombardi: "He possesses minimal football knowledge. Lacks motivation."

- Socrates was called, "An immoral corrupter of youth."

- When Peter J. Daniel was in the fourth grade, his teacher, Miss Phillips, constantly said, "Peter J. Daniel, you're no good, you're a bad apple and you're never going to amount to anything." Peter was virtually illiterate until he was 26. A friend stayed up with him all night and read him a copy of Think and Grow Rich. Now he owns the street corners he used to fight on and just published his latest book: Miss Phillips, You Were Wrong!

- Louisa May Alcott, the author of Little Women, was encouraged to find work as a servant or seamstress by her family.

- Beethoven handled the violin awkwardly and preferred playing his own compositions instead of improving his technique. His teacher called him hopeless as a composer.

- The parents of the famous opera singer Enrico Caruso wanted him to be an engineer. His teacher said he had no voice at all and could not sing.

- Charles Darwin, father of the theory of evolution, gave up a medical career and was told by his father, "You care for nothing but shooting, dogs and rat catching."

In his autobiography, Darwin wrote, "I was considered by all my masters and by my father, a very ordinary boy, rather below the common standard in intellect."

- Walt Disney was fired by a newspaper editor for lack of ideas. Walt Disney also went bankrupt before he built Disneyland.

- Thomas Edison's teachers said he was too stupid to learn anything.

- Albert Einstein did not speak until he was four years old and didn't read until he was seven. His teacher described him as "mentally slow, unsociable and adrift forever in his foolish dreams." He was expelled and was refused admittance to the Zurich Polytechnic School.

- Louis Pasteur was only a mediocre pupil in undergraduate studies and ranked 15th out of 22 in chemistry.

- Isaac Newton did very poorly in grade school.

- The sculptor Rodin's father said, "I have

an idiot for a son." Described as the worst pupil in the school, Rodin failed three times to secure admittance to the school of art. His uncle called him uneducable.

- Leo Tolstoy, author of War and Peace, flunked out of college. He was described as "both unable and unwilling to learn."

- Playwright Tennessee Williams was enraged when his play Me, Vasha was not chosen in a class competition at Washington University where he was enrolled in English XVI. The teacher recalled that Williams denounced the judges' choices and their intelligence.

- F. W. Woolworth's employers at the dry goods store said he had not enough sense to wait upon customers.

- Henry Ford failed and went broke five times before he finally succeeded.

- Babe Ruth, considered by sports historians to be the greatest athlete of all time and famous for setting the home run record, also holds the record for strikeouts.

- Winston Churchill failed sixth grade. He did not become Prime Minister of England until he was 66, and then only after a lifetime of defeats and setbacks. His greatest contributions came when he was a "senior citizen."

- Eighteen publishers turned down Richard Bach's 10,000-word story about a "soaring" seagull, *Jonathan Livingston Seagull*, before Macmillan finally published it in 1970. By 1975 it had sold more than 7 million copies in the U.S. alone.

- Richard Hooker worked for seven years on his humorous war novel, M*A*S*H, only to have it rejected by more than a dozen publishers before Morrow decided to publish it. It became a runaway best-seller, spawning a blockbuster movie and a highly successful television series.

~Jack Canfield and Mark Victor Hansen

Failure? No!
Just Temporary Setbacks

If you could come to my office in California to visit with me today, you would notice across one side of the room a beautiful old-fashioned Spanish tile and mahogany soda fountain with nine leather-covered stools (the kind they used to have in the old drugstores). Unusual? Yes. But if those stools could speak, they would tell you a story about the day I almost lost hope and gave up.

It was a recession period after World War II and jobs were scarce. Cowboy Bob, my husband, had purchased a small dry cleaning business with borrowed money. We had two darling babies, a tract home, a car and all the usual time payments. Then the bottom fell out. There was no money for the house payments or anything else.

I felt that I had no special talent, no training, no college education. I didn't think much of myself. But I remembered someone in my past who thought I had a little ability — my Alhambra High School English teacher. She inspired me to take journalism and named me advertising manager and feature editor of the school paper. I thought, "Now if I could write a 'Shoppers Column' for the small weekly newspaper in our rural town, maybe I could earn that house payment."

I had no car and no babysitter. So I pushed my two children before me in a rickety baby stroller with a big pillow tied in the back. The wheel kept coming off, but I hit it back on with the heel of my shoe and kept going. I was determined that my children would not lose their home as I often had done as a child.

But at the newspaper office, there were no jobs available. Recession. So I caught an idea. I asked if I might buy advertising space at wholesale and sell it at retail as a "Shoppers

Column." They agreed, telling me later that they mentally gave me about a week of pushing that beat-up heavily laden stroller down those country roads before I gave up. But they were wrong.

The newspaper column idea worked. I made enough money for the house payment and to buy an old used car that Cowboy Bob found for me. Then I hired a high school girl to babysit from three to five each afternoon. When the clock struck three, I grabbed my newspaper samples and flew out of the door to drive to my appointments.

But on one dark rainy afternoon every advertising prospect I had worked on turned me down when I went to pick up their copy.

"Why?" I asked. They said they had noticed that Ruben Ahlman, the President of the Chamber of Commerce and the owner of the Rexall drugstore did not advertise with me. His store was the most popular in town. They respected his judgment. "There must be something wrong with your advertising," they explained.

My heart sank. Those four ads would have made the house payment. Then I thought, I will try to speak with Mr. Ahlman one more time. Everyone loves and respects him. Surely he will listen. Every time I had tried to approach him in the past, he had refused to see me. He was always "out" or unavailable. I knew that if he advertised with me, the other merchants in town would follow his lead.

This time, as I walked into the Rexall drugstore, he was there at the prescription counter in the back. I smiled my best smile and held up my precious "Shoppers Column" carefully marked in my children's green Crayola. I said, "Everyone respects your opinion, Mr. Ahlman. Would you just look at my work for a moment so that I can tell the other merchants what you think?"

His mouth turned into in an upside down U. Without saying a word he emphatically shook his head, "NO!"

Suddenly all of my enthusiasm left me. I made it as far as the beautiful old soda fountain at the front of the drugstore, feeling that I didn't have the strength to drive home. I didn't want to sit at the soda fountain without buying something, so I pulled out my last dime and ordered a cherry Coke. I wondered desperately what to do. Would my babies lose their home as I had so many times when I was growing up? Was my journalism teacher wrong? Maybe that talent she talked about was just a dud. My eyes filled with tears.

A soft voice beside me on the next soda fountain stool said, "What is the matter, dear?" I looked up into the sympathetic face of a lovely gray-haired lady. I poured out my story to her, ending it with, "But Mr. Ahlman, who everyone respects so much, will not look at my work."

"Let me see that Shoppers Column," she said. She took my marked issue of the newspaper in her hands and carefully read it all the way through. Then she spun around on the stool, stood up, looked back at the prescription counter and in a commanding voice that could be heard down the block, said, "Ruben Ahlman, come *here!*" The lady was Mrs. Ahlman!

She told Ruben to buy the advertising from me. His mouth turned up the other way in a big grin. Then she asked me for the names of the four merchants who had turned me down. She went to the phone and called each one. She gave me a hug and told me they were waiting for me and to go back and pick up their ads.

Ruben and Vivian Ahlman became our dear friends, as well as steady advertising customers. I learned that Ruben was a darling man who bought from everyone. He had promised Vivian not to buy any more advertising. He was just trying to keep his word to her. If I had only asked others in town, I might have learned that I should have been talking to Mrs. Ahlman from the beginning. That conversation on the stools of the soda fountain was the turning point. My advertising business prospered and grew into four offices, with 285 employees serving 4,000 continuous-contract advertising accounts.

Later when Mr. Ahlman modernized the old drugstore and removed the soda fountain, my sweet husband Bob bought it and installed it in my office. If you were here in California, we would sit on the soda fountain stools together. I'd pour you a cherry Coke and remind you to never give up, to remember that help is always closer than we know.

Then I would tell you that if you can't communicate with a key person, search for more information. Try another path around. Look for someone who can communicate for you in a third person endorsement. And, finally, I would serve you these sparkling, refreshing words of Bill Marriott of the Marriott Hotels:

Failure? I never encountered it.

All I ever met were temporary setbacks.

~Dottie Walters

Take a Moment to Really See

We have all heard the expression: "Remember to stop and smell the roses." But, how often do we really take time out of our hectic fast-paced lives to notice the world around us? Too often we get caught up in our busy schedules, thoughts of our next appointment, the traffic or life in general, to even realize there are other people nearby.

I am as guilty as anyone of tuning out the world in this manner, especially when I am driving on California's overcrowded streets. A short time ago, however, I witnessed an event that showed me how being wrapped up in my own little world has kept me from being fully aware of the bigger world picture around me.

I was driving to a business appointment and, as usual, I was planning in my mind what

I was going to say. I came to a very busy intersection where the stoplight had just turned
red. "All right," I thought to myself, "I can beat
the next light if I race ahead of the pack."

My mind and car were on autopilot, ready
to go, when suddenly my trance was broken
by an unforgettable sight. A young couple,
both blind, were walking arm-in-arm across
this busy intersection with cars whizzing by in
every direction. The man was holding the
hand of a little boy, while the woman was
clutching a baby sling to her chest, obviously
carrying a child. Each of them had a white cane
extended, searching for clues to navigate them
across the intersection.

Initially I was moved. They were overcom-
ing what I felt was one of the most feared
handicaps — blindness. "Wouldn't it be terrible to be blind?" I thought. My thought was
quickly interrupted by horror when I saw that
the couple was not walking in the crosswalk,
but was instead veering diagonally, directly
toward the middle of the intersection. Without

realizing the danger they were in, they were walking right smack into the path of oncoming cars. I was frightened for them because I didn't know if the other drivers understood what was happening.

As I watched from the front line of traffic (I had the best seat in the house), I saw a miracle unfold before my eyes. *Every* car in *every* direction came to a simultaneous stop. I never heard the screech of brakes or even the peep of a car horn. Nobody even yelled, "Get out of the way!" Everything froze. In that moment, time seemed to stand still for this family.

Amazed, I looked at the cars around me to verify that we were all seeing the same thing. I noticed that everyone's attention was also fixed on the couple. Suddenly the driver to my right reacted. Craning his head out of his car, he yelled, "To your right. To your right!" Other people followed in unison, shouting, "To your right!"

Never skipping a beat, the couple adjusted their course as they followed the coaching.

Trusting their white canes and the calls from some concerned citizens, they made it to the other side of the road. As they arrived at the curb, one thing struck me — they were still arm-in-arm.

I was taken aback by the emotionless expressions on their faces and judged that they had no idea what was really going on around them. Yet I immediately sensed the sighs of relief exhaled by everyone stopped at that intersection.

As I glanced into the cars around me, the driver on my right was mouthing the words "Whew, did you see that?" The driver to the left of me was saying, "I can't believe it!" I think all of us were deeply moved by what we had just witnessed. Here were human beings stepping outside themselves for a moment to help four people in need.

I have reflected back on this situation many times since it happened and have learned several powerful lessons from it. The first is: "Slow down and smell the roses." (Something

I had rarely done up until then.) Take time to look around and really see what is going on in front of you right now. Do this and you will realize that this moment is all there is; more importantly, this moment is all that you have to make a difference in life.

The second lesson I learned is that the goals we set for ourselves can be attained through faith in ourselves and trust in others, despite seemingly insurmountable obstacles.

The blind couple's goal was simply to get to the other side of the road intact. Their obstacle was eight lanes of cars aimed straight at them. Yet, without panic or doubt, they walked forward until they reached their goal.

We too can move forward in attaining our goals, putting blinders on to the obstacles that would stand in our way. We just need to trust our intuition and accept the guidance of others who may have greater insight.

Finally, I learned to really appreciate my gift of sight, something I had taken for granted all too often.

Can you imagine how different life would be without your eyes? Try to imagine for a moment, walking into a busy intersection without being able to see. How often we forget the simple yet incredible gifts we have in our life.

As I drove away from that busy intersection, I did so with more awareness of life and compassion for others than I had arrived there with. Since then I have made the decision to really see life as I go about my daily activities and use my God-given talents to help others less fortunate.

Do yourself a favor as you walk through life: Slow down and take the time to really *see*. Take a moment to see what is going on around you right now, right where you are. You may be missing something wonderful.

~*Jeffrey Michael Thomas*

All I Remember

When my father spoke to me, he always began the conversation with "Have I told you yet today how much I adore you?" The expression of love was reciprocated and, in his later years, as his life began to visibly ebb, we grew even closer... if that were possible.

At 82 he was ready to die, and I was ready to let him go so that his suffering would end. We laughed and cried and held hands and told each other of our love and agreed that it was time. I said, "Dad, after you've gone I want a sign from you that you're fine." He laughed at the absurdity of that; Dad didn't believe in reincarnation. I wasn't positive I did either, but I had had many experiences that convinced me I could get some signal "from the other side."

My father and I were so deeply connected

I felt his heart attack in my chest at the moment he died. Later I mourned that the hospital staff, in their sterile wisdom, had not let me hold his hand as he had slipped away.

Day after day I prayed to hear from him, but nothing happened. Night after night I asked for a dream before I fell asleep. And yet four long months passed and I heard and felt nothing but grief at his loss. Mother had died five years before of Alzheimer's, and, though I had grown daughters of my own, I felt like a lost child.

One day, while I was lying on a massage table in a dark quiet room waiting for my appointment, a wave of longing for my father swept over me. I began to wonder if I had been too demanding in asking for a sign from him. I noticed that my mind was in a hyper acute state. I experienced an unfamiliar clarity in which I could have added long columns of figures in my head. I checked to make sure I was awake and not dreaming, and I saw that I was as far removed from a dreamy state as one could possibly be. Each thought I had was like a drop of water disturbing a still pond, and I marveled at the peacefulness of each passing moment. Then I thought, "I've been trying to control the messages from the other side; I will stop that now."

Suddenly my mother's face appeared — my mother, as she had been before Alzheimer's disease had stripped her of her mind, her humanity and 50 pounds. Her magnificent silver hair crowned her sweet face. She was so real and so close I felt I could reach out and touch her. She looked as she had a dozen years ago, before the wasting away had begun. I even smelled the fragrance of Joy, her favorite perfume. She seemed to be waiting and did not speak. I wondered how it could happen that I was thinking of my father and my mother appeared, and I felt a little guilty that I had not asked for her as well.

I said, "Oh, Mother, I'm so sorry that you had to suffer with that horrible disease."

She tipped her head slightly to one side, as

though to acknowledge what I had said about her suffering. Then she smiled — a beautiful smile — and said very distinctly, "But all I remember is love." And she disappeared.

I began to shiver in a room suddenly gone cold, and I knew in my bones that the love we give and receive is all that matters and all that is remembered. Suffering disappears; love remains.

Her words are the most important I have ever heard, and that moment is forever engraved on my heart.

I have not yet seen or heard from my father, but I have no doubt that someday, when I least expect it, he will appear and say, "Have I told you yet today that I love you?"

~Bobbie Probstein

Big Ed

When I arrived in the city to present a seminar on Tough-Minded Management, a small group of people took me to dinner to brief me on the people I would talk to the next day.

The obvious leader of the group was Big Ed, a large burly man with a deep rumbling voice. At dinner he informed me that he was a troubleshooter for a huge international organization. His job was to go into certain divisions or subsidiaries to terminate the employment of the executive in charge.

"Joe," he said, "I'm really looking forward to tomorrow because all of the guys need to listen to a tough guy like you. They're gonna find out that my style is the right one." He grinned and winked.

I smiled. I knew the next day was going to

be different from what he was anticipating.

The next day he sat impassively all through the seminar and left at the end without saying anything to me.

Three years later I returned to that city to present another management seminar to approximately the same group. Big Ed was there again. At about ten o'clock he suddenly stood up and asked loudly, "Joe, can I say something to these people?"

I grinned and said, "Sure. When anybody is as big as you are, Ed, he can say anything he wants."

Big Ed went on to say, "All of you guys know me and some of you know what's happened to me. I want to share it, however, with all of you. Joe, I think you'll appreciate it by the time I've finished.

"When I heard you suggest that each of us, in order to become really tough-minded, needed to learn to tell those closest to us that we really loved them, I thought it was a bunch of sentimental garbage. I wondered what in the world that had to do with being tough. You had said toughness is like leather, and hardness is like granite, that the tough mind is open, resilient, disciplined and tenacious. But I couldn't see what love had to do with it.

"That night, as I sat across the living room from my wife, your words were still bugging me. What kind of courage would it take to tell my wife I loved her? Couldn't anybody do it? You had also said this should be in the daylight and not in the bedroom. I found myself clearing my throat and starting and then stopping. My wife looked up and asked me what I had said, and I answered, 'Oh nothing.' Then suddenly, I got up, walked across the room, nervously pushed her newspaper aside and said, 'Alice, I love you.' For a minute she looked startled. Then the tears came to her eyes and she said softly, 'Ed, I love you, too, but this is the first time in 25 years you've said it like that.'

"We talked a while about how love, if there's enough of it, can dissolve all kinds of tensions, and suddenly I decided on the spur of the moment to call my older son in New York. We have never really communicated well. When I got him on the phone, I blurted out, 'Son, you're liable to think I'm drunk, but I'm not. I just thought I'd call you and tell you I love you.'

"There was a pause at his end and then I heard him say quietly, 'Dad, I guess I've known that, but it's sure good to hear. I want you to know I love you, too.' We had a good chat and then I called my younger son in San Francisco. We had been closer. I told him the same thing and this, too, led to a real fine talk like we'd never really had.

"As I lay in bed that night thinking, I realized that all the things you'd talked about that day — real management nuts and bolts — took on extra meaning, and I could get a handle on how to apply them if I really understood and practiced tough-minded love.

"I began to read books on the subject. Sure enough, Joe, a lot of great people had a lot to say, and I began to realize the enormous practicality of applied love in my life, both at home and at work.

"As some of you guys here know, I really changed the way I work with people. I began to listen more and to really hear. I learned what it was like to try to get to know people's strengths rather than dwelling on their weaknesses. I began to discover the real pleasure of helping build their confidence. Maybe the most important thing of all was that I really began to understand that an excellent way to show love and respect for people was to expect them to use their strengths to meet objectives we had worked out together.

"Joe, this is my way of saying thanks. Incidentally, talk about practical! I'm now executive vice-president of the company and they call me a pivotal leader. Okay, you guys, now listen to this guy!"

~Joe Batten

Meet Our Contributors

Joe Batten, C.P.A.E., is a professional speaker and a successful businessperson who knows how to inspire confidence in organizations in good economic times and bad. His 35 years as an author, consultant and speaker have earned him the title of Corporate Mentor. Joe wrote the bestselling book: *Tough Minded Management.* Joe is a man who loves life and laughter and translates that warmth and passion to every audience. You can reach Joe by writing to 4505 S.W. 26th St., Des Moines, IA 50321-2813. Call (515) 285-8069 or fax (515) 285-5672.

Gene Bedley is a retired principal, recipient of the PTA's 1985 National Educator of the Year Award and the Milken Family Foundation's 1994 Educator of the Year, and author of numerous books on creating a positive classroom environment. He can be reached at 14252 East Mall, Irvine, California 92714 or call (714) 551-6690.

Helice Bridges is a recognized and dynamic speaker and trainer who travels internationally doing self-esteem training and workshops for schools, organizations and businesses. She is Chairperson of the Board for Difference Makers, Inc. and can be reached at P.O. Box 2115, Del Mar, California 92014 or call (800) 887-8422 or (760) 634-1851

Stan Dale, formerly the voice of "The Shadow" and the announcer/narrator of "The Lone Ranger," "Sgt. Preston" and "The Green Hornet" radio shows, is the Director/Founder of the Human Awareness Institute in San Mateo, California, an organization dedicated to "creating a world where everyone wins." He conducts "Sex, Love and Intimacy Workshops" around the world. Stan is the author of *Fantasies Can Set You Free* and *My Child, My*

Self: How To Raise The Child You Always Wanted To Be. Both books are also available on cassette from The Human Awareness Institute, 1720 S. Amphlett Blvd., Suite 128, San Mateo, California 94402 or call (800) 800-4117 or (415) 571-5524.

Rick Gelinas is the President of the Lucky Acorns Delphi Foundation in Miami Florida. He is a master educator and has dedicated his life to making a difference to children. You can reach him at 5888 S.W. 77 Terrace, Miami Florida 33143 or call (305) 667-7756.

Robert A. Moawad is Chairman and Chief Executive Officer of Edge Learning Institute with offices in Tacoma, Washington, and Tempe, Arizona. Edge is a professional development firm dedicated to assisting organizations achieve greater levels of productivity, quality and customer satisfaction. Bob is a dynamic "edu-tainer." He has an impressive ability to inspire and have an impact on an audience by blending colorful illustrations with solid principles. This has made Bob one of the most sought-after keynote speakers in the nation. Since 1973 he has assisted more than two million people, including some of the most respected leaders in business, government and education. He can be contacted by writing Edge Learning Institute, 2217 N. 30th, #200, Tacoma, Washington 98403 or call (206) 272-3103.

Michael J. Murphy, Ed.D., DFP, is a family therapist and author of *Popsicle Fish and Other Fathering Stories.* For information or presentations, contact The Family Consultation Team, 349 Old Plymouth Road, P.O. Box 300, Sagamore Beach, MA 02562 or call (508) 833-3800.

Bobbie Probstein is a writer and photographer whose new book, *Healing Now*, has been widely praised. It is invaluable for anyone affected by illness or preparing for surgery. Her first book, an autobiography, *Return* *to Center*, is in its third printing. She may be reached at 28 Shoal Dr., Corona Del Mar, CA 92625.

Jeffrey Michael Thomas is a regional vice-president for Van Kampen Merritt, a professional money management firm. He is a member of the National Speakers Association and speaks on topics ranging from financial management to fundraising for various charities through his company, J. Michael Thomas & Associates. Mr. Thomas lives and works in Tustin, California, and he is currently seeking a seat on the Tustin City Council. He can be reached at (714) 544-1352.

Dottie Walters is President of the Walters International Speakers Bureau in California. She sends paid speakers all over the world and is heavily involved in presentation training. She is the author, with her daughter Lilly, of the new Simon and Schuster book, *Speak And Grow Rich*, and is founder and administrator of the International Group of Agents and Bureaus. Dottie publishes Sharing Ideas, the largest news magazine in the world for paid professional speakers. You can write her at P.O. Box 1120, Glendora, California 91740 or call (818) 335-8069 or fax (818) 335-6127.

Meet Our Authors

Jack Canfield is the co-creator of the *Chicken Soup for the Soul* series, which *Time* magazine has called "the publishing phenomenon of the decade." Jack is also the co-author of many other bestselling books.

Jack is the CEO of the Canfield Training Group in Santa Barbara, California, and founder of the Foundation for Self-Esteem in Culver City, California. He has conducted intensive personal and professional development seminars on the principles of success for more than a million people in twenty-three countries, has spoken to hundreds of thousands of people at more than 1,000 corporations, universities, professional conferences and conventions, and has been seen by millions more on national television shows.

Jack has received many awards and honors,

including three honorary doctorates and a Guinness World Records Certificate for having seven books from the *Chicken Soup for the Soul* series appearing on the *New York Times* bestseller list on May 24, 1998.

You can reach Jack at
www.jackcanfield.com.

Mark Victor Hansen is the co-founder of Chicken Soup for the Soul, along with Jack Canfield. He is a sought-after keynote speaker, bestselling author, and marketing maven. Mark's powerful messages of possibility, opportunity, and action have created powerful change in thousands of organizations and millions of individuals worldwide.

Mark is a prolific writer with many bestselling books in addition to the *Chicken Soup for the Soul* series. Mark has had a profound influence in the field of human potential through his library of audios, videos, and articles in the areas of big thinking, sales achievement, wealth building, publishing success, and personal and professional development. He is also the founder of the MEGA Seminar Series.

Mark has received numerous awards that honor his entrepreneurial spirit, philanthropic heart, and business acumen. He is a lifetime member of the Horatio Alger Association of Distinguished Americans.

You can reach Mark at
www.markvictorhansen.com.

Amy Newmark was a writer, speaker, Wall Street analyst and business executive in the worlds of finance and telecommunications for more than thirty years. Today she is publisher, editor-in-chief and coauthor of the Chicken Soup for the Soul book series. By curating and editing inspirational true stories from ordinary people who have had extraordinary experiences, Amy has kept the twenty-one-year-old Chicken Soup for the Soul brand fresh and relevant, and still part of the social zeitgeist.

Amy graduated *magna cum laude* from Harvard University where she majored in Portuguese and minored in French. She wrote her thesis about popular, spoken-word poetry in Brazil, which involved traveling throughout Brazil and meeting with poets and writers to collect their stories. She is delighted to have come full circle in her writing career—from collecting poetry "from the people" in Brazil as a twenty-year-old to, three decades later, collecting stories and poems "from the people" for Chicken Soup for the Soul.

Amy has a national syndicated newspaper column and is a frequent radio and TV guest, passing along the real-life lessons and useful tips she has picked up from reading and editing thousands of Chicken Soup for the Soul stories.

She and her husband are the proud parents of four grown children and in her limited spare time, Amy enjoys visiting them, hiking, and reading books that she did not have to edit.

Sharing Happiness, Inspiration, and Wellness

Real people sharing real stories, every day, all over the world. In 2007, *USA Today* named *Chicken Soup for the Soul* one of the five most memorable books in the last quarter-century. With over 100 million books sold to date in the U.S. and Canada alone, more than 200 titles in print, and translations into more than forty languages, "chicken soup for the soul" is one of the world's best-known phrases.

Today, twenty-one years after we first began sharing happiness, inspiration and wellness through our books, we continue to delight our readers with new titles, but have also evolved beyond the bookstore, with wholesome and balanced pet food, delicious nutritious comfort food, and a major motion picture in development. Whatever you're doing, wherever you are, Chicken Soup for the Soul is "always there for you™." Thanks for reading!

Share with Us

We all have had Chicken Soup for the Soul moments in our lives. If you would like to share your story or poem with millions of people around the world, go to chickensoup.com and click on "Submit Your Story." You may be able to help another reader, and become a published author at the same time. Some of our past contributors have launched writing and speaking careers from the publication of their stories in our books!

We only accept story submissions via our website. They are no longer accepted via mail or fax.

To contact us regarding other matters, please send us an e-mail through webmaster@chickensoupforthesoul.com, or fax or write us at:

Chicken Soup for the Soul
P.O. Box 700
Cos Cob, CT 06807-0700
Fax: 203-861-7194

One more note from your friends at Chicken Soup for the Soul: Occasionally, we receive an unsolicited book manuscript from one of our readers, and we would like to respectfully inform you that we do not accept unsolicited manuscripts and we must discard the ones that appear.